# Poetry Pro

## Grades 1-3

**Written by Ruth Solski**
**Illustrated by S&S Learning Materials**

**ISBN 1-55035-831-6**
**Copyright 2006**
**All Rights Reserved * Printed in Canada**

Published in the United States by:
On the Mark Press
3909 Witmer Road  PMB 175
Niagara Falls, New York
14305
www.onthemarkpress.com

Published in Canada by:
S&S Learning Materials
15 Dairy Avenue
Napanee, Ontario
K7R 1M4
www.sslearning.com

# At  Glance™

| Learning Expectations | Section 1 | Section 2 | Section 3 | Section 4 | Section 5 | Section 6 | Section 7 | Section 8 |
|---|---|---|---|---|---|---|---|---|
| **Literacy Skills** | | | | | | | | |
| • Developing Poetry Appreciation | • | • | • | • | • | • | • | • |
| • Reading Different Forms of Poetry | • | • | • | • | • | • | • | • |
| • Dramatizing Poetry Through Choral Reading | • | | | | | | | |
| • Identifying Rhyme | | • | | | | | | |
| • Listening For Rhyme | | • | | | | | | |
| • Using Word Families in Rhymes | | • | | | | | | |
| • Implementing Rhyming Words to Form Rhymes | | • | | | | | | |
| • Learning About and Creating Poetry Forms | | | • | • | • | • | • | • |
| • Rhyming Couplets | | | • | | | | | |
| • Two Word Poetry | | | | • | | | | |
| • Acrostic Poetry | | | | | • | | | |
| • Limericks | | | | | | • | | |
| • Haiku | | | | | | | • | |
| • Cinquain | | | | | | | | • |

# Poetry Prompts

# Table Of Contents

# Writing Poetry

# Teacher Assessment Rubric

**Student's Name:** _____

| Criteria | Level 1 | Level 2 | Level 3 | Level 4 |
|---|---|---|---|---|
| **Listening Skills** | Listens to poetry for only a short time | Listens to poetry for some of the time | Listens to poetry most of the time | Listens well and understands the theme |
| **Rhyming Words** | Hears and identifies a few of the words | Hears and identifies some of the words | Hears and identifies most of the words | Hears and identifies all of the words |
| **Rhyming Couplets** | Forms a rhyming couplet with a lot of help | Forms a rhyming couplet with some help | Forms a simple rhyming couplet | Forms a rhyming couplet independently |
| **Writing Poetry** | Is not able to write poetry independently | Is able to write poetry with some help | Is able to write simple forms of poetry | Is able to write the forms taught independently |
| **Poetry Appreciation** | Seldom reads a poem | Reads a poem some of the time | Reads and enjoys most poems | Reads and enjoys all forms of poetry |

Comments:

_____

_____

_____

_____

_____

_____

_____

_____

# Writing Poetry

## Student Self-Assessment Rubric

Name: _____

Put a check mark ✓ in the box that best describes you.

| | Always ★★★★ | Almost Always ★★★ | Sometimes ★★ | Needs Improvement ★ |
|---|---|---|---|---|
| ✓ I am a good listener. | | | | |
| ✓ I follow instructions and finish work on time. | | | | |
| ✓ I know what rhyming words are. | | | | |
| ✓ I can write a rhyming couplet. | | | | |
| ✓ I can express my feelings and ideas in a poem. | | | | |
| ✓ I can read a poem with good expression. | | | | |

1. I liked _____

_____

2. I learned _____

_____

3. I want to learn _____

_____

# Introduction

Poetry is a literary art form that is often forgotten about in the classroom. Young students sometimes experience great difficulty writing any form of poetry. Hopefully the ideas and activities in this book will provide you with some easy ways to introduce poetry writing to your students. You will find guidance in reading, appreciating and writing a variety of poetry forms.

The "What is Poetry" section establishes the base for poetry writing. It stresses the importance of listening to and the reading of poetry in the classroom on a regular basis. Choral reading is promoted and explained how to use with your students. This section also contains twenty nursery rhymes and ten rhyming poems divided into parts for choral reading.

Rhyming skills are reviewed in the "Rhyming Words" section. In this section you will find Word Family Lists, ideas to recall rhyming skills, ear training and listening skills and an assortment of rhyming activities and worksheets.

Poetry writing development ideas are located in the "Traditional Poetry" section. Here you will find ways to teach and practice writing rhyming couplets, two word poetry, acrostic poetry, limericks, haiku and cinquains.

This book has been developed to inspire your students to achieve a greater appreciation for poetry and to supplement your own good ideas for teaching this genre. The activities are designed to make poetry writing a pleasurable and successful experience for you and your students.

# What is Poetry ?

Poetry is a form of literature in which the sound and meaning of language are combined to create ideas and feelings. In today's society poetry is everywhere. It is found in the lyrics of songs, heard in television commercials, radio jingles, written in greeting cards, and said in jump rope chants.

> See the cat
>
> On the mat.
>
> It is fat
>
> Said the rat.

People are attracted by the sound and rhythm of a poem's words. Poetry comes in all shapes and sizes. Poems are filled with feelings, ideas, moods, topics and stories. Children enjoy the pleasing rhythms found in nursery rhymes. They will clap their hands and move their bodies to the rhythm of the language.

Poetry began in prehistoric times. Poetic language was used by early people in songs, prayers and magic spells. The pattern of rhyme and rhythm helped people to remember and preserve oral poetry from generation to generation.

## Listening to Poetry

In order for children to develop a "poetic ear", they should hear poetry often. Poetry can be integrated throughout many subject areas in your school's curriculum. Poems should be visible. They should be printed on chart paper and posted on the chalkboard, bulletin boards, walls and doors. The poems should be read by the teacher and the topic discussed with the students. Clap its rhythm, look for interesting words and rhyming words. Please do not overdo the discussion. Listening to and reading poetry should be pleasurable.

## How to Read a Poem

When students first read a poem it should be read carefully all the way through silently. Then it should be read aloud by the class. Draw the students attention to the punctuation mark at the end of each line or the absence of one. If there is punctuation there should be a slight pause. When there is no punctuation at the end of the line, instruct your students to continue on to the next line. Practice reading poems with your students to improve and strengthen reading skills, oral expression and to further their appreciation for this literary art form.

Section 1

Write the following poem on a chart.

# A Tale About A Cottontail.....

A pink-eared bunny
With a white, white tail,
Was hopping along
On a woodland trail,
When a wee little mouse
With bright, bright eyes,
Called out to him, "Bunny,
Take care! Be wise!
Look out for the fox
By the still, still brook!"
But the foolish young bunny
Didn't listen or look;
He just wrinkled up
His pink, pink nose,
The way bunnies do,
As everyone knows,
And said as he waved
His long, long ears,
"Run away, little man,
With your mousey fears."
And he hopped right along
To his sad, sad end.
Don't you wish he had listened
To his wise little friend?

# Choral Reading

Choral reading is as old as poetry itself. It was one of the earliest forms of artistic expression used during festivals and religious rites of primitive people before it was used in the presentation of dramatic ideas in the theater. It is still used today for ritualistic purposes in congregational reading of psalms and other liturgical literature in church worship.

Choral reading is a delightful way for children to read aloud poetry in school. At the same time it will develop an appreciation of different forms of poetry as well as promote and strengthen reading with expression. This type of group reading provides a unique social experience shared by all students.

Section 1

# Classroom Choral Reading

1. Select a poem that your students will be able to read and memorize easily. For the early grades I suggest you begin with a nursery rhyme or an easy four line poem.

2. Record the poem on a chart. Mark the lines to be spoken by one person or a group with a different color.

3. Read the poem aloud to the students with good expression and clear enunciation. Use your pointer or hand to demonstrate the flow and rhythm as you read.

4. Discuss the topic, mood, descriptive vocabulary and the rhyming words in the poem.

5. Underline the rhyming words. Brainstorm for other words that rhyme with the ones in the poem.

6. Read the poem again and have the children hand clap, tap one foot, and move their bodies to the rhythm of the piece.

7. Over a period of time have the students practice saying the poem. Cover up one line of the poem at a time until everyone is able to recite it from memory.

8. Actions could be added to facilitate memorization. They could be dropped later.

9. Once the students have mastered one poem, lead them on to the next one. Try to implement one or two poems per month into your program. Always review the ones previously learned.

10. Memorization is a lost art but is a very necessary skill for students to have in order to recall addition, subtraction and multiplication facts; historical and scientific facts; spelling words. It is a sense of great satisfaction in one's later years to recite poetry and tell stories that one has learned as a child.

# Choral Reading

Choral reading is a great art form that can be used for class presentations at school concerts and for special events. It promotes team work in a performance atmosphere.

# Special Devices

In a piece chosen for choral speaking, students may be chosen to perform solos, duets, trios, quartets, quintets, by rows and alternate reading by boys and girls.

Section 1

# The Solo

The solo device in choral reading serves two specific purposes. First, it provides for the first personal pronoun or what would be the speaker.

**Example:**

I'm a little apple *(Solo)*
Red and round *(All)*
From the treetop *(All)*
I fell down *(Solo)*
Please pick it up *(All)*
And take it home *(All)*
I don't want to *(Solo)*
Stay alone *(Solo)*

The solo is also used to call attention to each of the following factors:

1.  the meaning of a particular line

2.  the abrupt introduction of a new idea or thought

3.  the expression of a subdued word

4.  a phrase

5.  a sentence

6.  deep feeling

7.  mock-seriousness

8.  the best possible means to give a number of different, individual students an opportunity to participate is an important function of reading.

# Poems For Choral Reading

## Nursery Rhymes

Use good old-fashioned nursery rhymes with younger students. Their simplicity and rhythm appeals to this age group. As the students become more proficient with choral reading introduce more difficult forms of traditional poetry.

### Baa, Baa Black Sheep

Baa, Baa, black sheep *(Solo 1)*
Have you any wool? *(All)*
Yes sir, yes sir, *(Solo 2)*
Three bags full: *(Solo 2)*

One for my master, *(Boy)*
One for my dame, *(Girl)*
But none for the little boy *(All)*
That lives down the lane. *(All)*

### Hickory Dickory Dock

Hickory, dickory dock. *(Girls)*
The mouse ran up the clock. *(Boys)*
The clock struck One, *(All)*
The mouse ran down, *(Boys)*
Hickory, dickory, dock. *(All)*
Tick tock. *(Solo)*

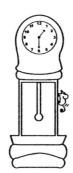

### Hey Diddle Diddle!

Hey diddle, diddle *(All)*
The cat and the fiddle, *(Girls)*
The cow jumped over the moon. *(Boys)*
The little dog laughed *(Solo)*
To see such sport *(Solo)*
And the dish ran away with the spoon! *(All)*

Section 1

# Humpty Dumpty

Humpty Dumpty sat on a wall. *(Girls)*
Humpty Dumpty had a great fall. *(Boys)*
All the King's horses *(Girls)*
And all the King's men *(Boys)*
Couldn't put Humpty together again. *(All)*

# Jack and Jill

Jack and Jill *(Girls)*
Went up the hill *(Boys)*
To fetch a pail of water; *(All)*
Jack fell down *(Solo 1)*
And broke his crown, *(Solo 2)*
And Jill came tumbling after. *(All)*

Up got Jack *(Solo 1)*
And home did trot *(Girls)*
As fast as he could caper. *(All)*
He went to bed to mend his head, *(Boys)*
With vinegar and brown paper. *(All)*

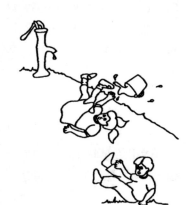

# One, Two, Buckle My Shoe

One, two, buckle my shoe, *(Girls)*
Three, four, shut the door, *(Boys)*
Five, six, pick up sticks, *(Girls)*
Seven, eight, lay them straight, *(Boys)*
Nine, ten, a big fat hen. *(All)*

# Little Miss Muffet

Little Miss Muffet *(Girls)*
Sat on a tuffet, *(Boys)*
Eating her curds and whey; *(All)*
Along came a spider *(Boys)*
And sat down beside her, *(Girls)*
And frightened Miss Muffet away. *(All)*

Section 1

# Little Boy Blue

Little Boy Blue, come blow your horn, *(Solo)*
The sheep's in the meadow *(Girls)*
The cow's in the corn. *(Boys)*
Where's the little boy *(Solo 1)*
That looks after the sheep? *(Solo 1)*
He's under the haystack fast asleep. *(Girls)*
Will you wake him? *(Solo 1)*
No not I; *(Solo 2)*
For if I do, he'll be sure to cry. *(Solo 2)*

# Little Jack Horner

Little Jack Horner *(Solo)*
Sat in a corner *(Girls)*
Eating a Christmas pie; *(Boys)*
He put in his thumb, *(Girls)*
And pulled out a plum, *(Boys)*
And said, *(Boys)*
"What a good boy am I." *(Solo)*

# Mistress Mary

Mistress Mary *(Girls)*
Quite contrary *(Boys)*
"How does your garden grow?" *(All)*
"With silverbells *(Solo 1)*
And cockle shells, *(Solo 2)*
And pretty maids, all in a row." *(All)*

# Lucy Locket

Luck Locket lost her pocket; *(Solo 1)*
Kity Fisher found it; *(Solo 2)*
But not a penny was inside, *(All)*
And only a binding round it. *(All)*

Section 1

# Mix a Pancake

Mix a pancake, *(Boys)*
Stir a pancake, *(Girls)*
Pop it in a pan; *(All)*
Fry the pancake, *(Girls)*
Toss the pancake, *(Boys)*
Catch it if you can. *(All)*

# Tom, Tom, The Piper's Son

Tom, Tom, the Piper's son, *(Solo 1)*
Stole a pig and away he run. *(Boys)*
The pig was eat *(Girls)*
And Tom was beat *(Boys)*
Which sent him howling down the street. *(All)*

# Some Little Mice

Some little mice sat in a barn to spin *(All)*
Pussy came by, *(Girls)* and popped her head in *(Boys)*
"Shall I come in and cut your threads off?" *(Solo)*
"Oh no, kind Pussy, *(Girls)* you may snap our
heads off." *(All)*

# Pease Porridge Hot

Pease porridge hot, *(Girls)*
Pease porridge cold, *(Boys)*
Pease porridge in the pot, *(All)*
Nine days old, *(All)*
Some like it hot, *(Girls)*
Some like it cold, *(Boys)*
But all like it in the pot, *(All)*
Nine days old. *(All)*

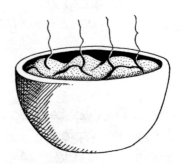

14

# Pat-A-Cake

Pat-a-cake, pat-a-cake, baker's man! *(All)*
Make me a cake as fast as you can. *(All)*
Pat it *(Solo 1)* and prick it, *(Solo 2)*
And mark it with a T, *(Solo 3)*
And bake it in the oven *(All)*
For Baby and me. *(All)*

# There Was a Crooked Man

There was a crooked man *(Girls)*
And he walked a crooked mile, *(Boys)*
He found a  crooked sixpence *(Girls)*
Against a crooked stile; *(All)*
He found a crooked cat, *(Boys)*
Which caught a crooked mouse, *(Girls)*
And they all lived together *(All)*
In a little crooked house. *(All)*

# Old King Cole

Old King Cole *(Solo 1)*
Was a merry old soul *(Girls)*
And a merry old soul was he; *(Boys)*
He called for his pipe *(Girls)*
And he called for his bowl, *(Boys)*
And he called for his fiddlers three. *(Trio)*
Every fiddler he had a fine fiddle, *(Boys)*
And a very fine fiddle had he; *(Girls)*
"Tweedle-dee, tweedle dee," went the fiddlers. *(Trio)*
Oh, there's none so rare, *(All)*
As can compare *(All)*
With King Cole and his fiddlers three. *(All)*

# I Had a Little Pony

I had a little pony, *(Solo 1)*
I called him Dapple Gray, *(Solo 2)*
I lent him to a lady *(Solo 3)*
To ride a mile away. *(All)*
She whipped him *(Girls)*, she lashed him *(Boys)*
She rode him through the mire, *(All)*
I would not lend my pony now *(Solo 1)*
For all the lady's hire. *(All)*

# Goosie Gander

Goosie, Goosie Gander *(Boys)*
Whither did you wander? *(Girls)*
Upstairs *(Boys)* and downstairs *(Girls)*
And in my lady's chamber. *(All)*
There I met an old man, *(Solo)*
Who would not say his prayers *(All)*
I took him by the left leg, *(Solo)*
And threw him down the stairs. *(All)*

# Little Bo-Peep

Little Bo-Peep has lost her sheep, *(Girls)*
And doesn't know where to find them; *(Boys)*
Leave them alone, *(Girls)* and they'll come home. *(Boys)*
Wagging their tails behind them. *(All)*

# To Market

To market, to market, to buy a fat pig, *(All)*
Home again, home again, jiggety jig. *(Girls)*
To market, to market, to buy a fat hog, *(All)*
Home again, home again, jiggety jog. *(Boys)*
To market, to market, to buy a plum bun *(All)*
Home again, home again, market is done *(All)*

Section 1

# Rhyming Poetry

## Dinosaur, Dinosaur

Dinosaur, Dinosaur, *(Boys)*
Where have you been? *(Girls)*
"I've been to the swamp *(Solo 1)*
To find plants delicious and green." *(Solo 1)*

Dinosaur, Dinosaur, *(Boys)*
What did you there? *(Girls)*
"I stood and I ate *(Solo 2)*
Until I had a terrible scare." *(Solo 2)*

Dinosaur, Dinosaur, *(Boys)*
What did you see? *(Girls)*
"I saw Tyrannosaurus Rex *(Solo 3)*
Coming after me!" *(Solo 3)*

Dinosaur, Dinosaur, *(Boys)*
Did you fight the great king? *(Girls)*
"No! Safe in the water I stood *(Solo 4)*
And laughed at the angry old thing" *(Solo 4)*

*R. Solski*

## Five Little Possums

Five Little Possums *(All)*
Sat in a tree *(All)*
The first one said *(Girls)*
"What do you see?" *(Solo 1)*
The second one said *(Boys)*
"A man with a gun." *(Solo 2)*
The third one said, *(Girls)*
"We'd better run," *(Solo 3)*
The fourth one said *(Boys)*
"Let's hide in the shade." *(Solo 4)*
The fifth one said, *(Girls)*
"I'm not afraid." *(Solo 5)*
Then BANG went the gun *(All)*
And how they did run! *(All)*

*Anonymous*

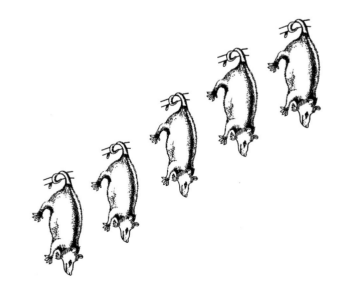

Section 1

# The Squirrel

Whisky, frisky, *(All)*
Hippity hop. *(All)*
Up he goes *(Girls)*
To the tree top. *(Girls)*

Whirly, twirly, *(All)*
Round and round, *(All)*
Down he scampers *(Boys)*
To the ground. *(Boys)*

Furly, curly, *(All)*
What a tail, *(All)*
Tall as a feather *(Girls)*
Broad as a sail. *(Girls)*

Where's his supper? *(Boys)*
In the shell, *(Girls)*
Snappity, crackity, *(All)*
Out it fell! *(All)*
                    *Anonymous*

# The Little Groundhog

See the fat, round Groundhog, *(Girls)*
All dressed in brown. *(Boys)*
Standing silent and still *(Girls)*
Looking all around. *(Boys)*
He looks to the left. *(Solo 1)*
He looks to the right. *(Solo 2)*
Suddenly he sees something *(All)*
That gives him a fright! *(All)*
Down his hole he quickly leaps *(Girls)*
Winter will last for six more weeks. *(Boys)*
                    *R. Solski*

Section 1

## Once I saw a Little Bird

Once I saw a little bird *(Solo 1)*
Come hop, hop, hop. *(All)*
So I cried, "Little bird," *(Solo 2)*
Will you stop, stop, stop?" *(All)*

I was going to the window *(Solo 1)*
To say, "How do you do?" *(Solo 2)*
But he shook his little tail, *(Boys)*
And away he flew. *(Girls)*

*Anonymous*

## The Chickens

Said the first, little chicken, *(Girls)*
With a queer, little squirm, *(Girls)*

"I wish I could find *(Solo 1)*
A fat, little worm." *(Solo 1)*

Said the next little chicken, *(Boys)*
With an odd, little shrug: *(Boys)*

I wish I could find *(Solo 2)*
A fat little bug." *(Solo 2)*

Said a third little chicken, *(Girls)*
With a small sigh of grief: *(Girls)*

"I wish I could find *(Solo 3)*
A little, green leaf!" *(Solo 3)*

Said the fourth little chicken, *(Boys)*
With a faint little moan: *(Boys)*

"I wish I could find *(Solo 4)*
A wee gravel stone." *(Solo 4)*

"Now, see here!" said the mother *(Solo 5)*
From the green garden patch, *(Girls)*

"If you want any breakfast, *(Solo 5)*
Just come here and scratch?" *(Solo 5)*

*Anonymous*

19

**Section 1**

# Where Do All the Daisies Go?

Where do all the daisies go? *(Teacher)*
I know! *(Boys)*, I know! *(Girls)*
Underneath the snow they creep, *(Girls)*
Nod their heads and sleep, *(Boys)*
In the springtime out they peep; *(Girls)*
That is where they go! *(All)*

Where do all the birdies go? *(Teacher)*
I know! *(Boys)*, I know! *(Girls)*
Far away from winter snow, *(All)*
To the fair, warm South they go. *(All)*
Where they stay till daisies blow; *(Girls)*
That is where they go! *(Boys)*

Where do all the babies go? *(Teacher)*
I Know! *(Boys)* I Know! *(Girls)*
In the glancing firelight warm, *(Boys)*
Safely sheltered from all harm. *(Girls)*
Softly they lie on mother's arm; *(All)*
That is where they go! *(All)*

*Anonymous*

# The Secret

We have a secret, just we three *(Trio)*
The robin, and I, and the sweet cherry tree; *(Trio)*
The bird told the tree, and the tree told me, *(All)*
And nobody knows it but just we three. *(Trio)*

But of course the robin knows it best, *(All)*
Because he built the ---------- I shan't tell the rest *(Solo 1)*
And laid the four little ---------- something in it ---------- *(All)*
I'm afraid I shall tell it every minute. *(Solo 2)*

But if the tree and the robin don't peep, *(All)*
I'll try my best the secret to keep; *(Solo 3)*
Though I know when the little birds fly about *(All)*
Then the whole secret will be out. *(All)*

*Anonymous*

Section 1

# Long, Long Ago

Wind through the olive trees *(All)*
Softly did blow. *(All)*
Round little Bethlehem *(Girls)*
Long, long ago. *(Boys)*

Sheep on the hillside lay *(Girls)*
Whiter than snow. *(Girls)*
Shepherds were watching them *(Boys)*
Long, long ago. *(Boys)*

Then from the happy sky *(Girls)*
Angels bent low. *(Girls)*
Singing their songs of joy *(Boys)*
Long, long ago. *(Boys)*

For in a manger bed *(All)*
Cradled we know, *(All)*
Christ came to Bethlehem *(All)*
Long, long ago. *(All)*
*Anonymous*

# October

October's very busy, *(Girls)*
Putting all the flowers to bed, *(Boys)*
And making warm, leaf blankets *(Girls)*
Of yellow, brown and red. *(Boys)*

She tucks the blanket snugly in, *(Girls)*
Then whispers to them all, *(Boys)*
Sleep safe and warm dear flowers, *(All)*
Until the March winds call. *(All)*
*Anonymous*

# Frost

Little Jack Frost comes as still as a mouse *(Boys)*
He paints all the windows of everyone's house; *(Girls)*
He pinches your nose, *(Girls)* and he pinches your toes, *(Boys)*
But he gives us the ice and the white sparkling snows; *(Solo 1)*
And without him much pleasure would surely be lost. *(Solo 2)*
Hurrah for the coming of little Jack Frost! *(All)*
*Anonymous*

Section 1

# The Friendly Beasts

Jesus our brother, kind and good, *(Boys)*
Was humbly born in a stable rude. *(Girls)*
The friendly beasts around him stood *(Boys)*
Jesus our brother, kind and good. *(Girls)*

"I," said the donkey, shaggy and brown *(Solo 1)*
"I," carried His mother up hill and down; *(Solo 1)*
"I," carried her safely to Bethlehem town, *(Solo 1)*
"I," said the donkey, shaggy and brown *(All)*

"I," said the cow, all white and red, *(Solo 2)*
"I," gave Him my manger for His bed; *(Solo 2)*
"I," gave Him my hay to pillow His head." *(Solo 2)*
"I," said the cow, all white and red. *(All)*

"I," said the sheep with curly horn, *(Solo 3)*
"I," gave Him wool for a blanket warm! *(Solo 3)*
"He wore my coat on Christmas morn." *(Solo 3)*
"I," said the sheep with the curly horn. *(All)*

"I," said the dove from the rafters high, *(Solo 4)*
"I," cooed Him to sleep so He would not cry", *(Solo 4)*
"I," cooed Him to sleep, my mate and I." *(Solo 4)*
"I," said the dove from the rafters high. *(All)*

And every beast, by some good spell, *(Girls)*
In the stable dark was glad to tell, *(Boys)*
Of the gift he gave Immanuel, *(All)*
The gift he gave Immanuel. *(All)*

*Anonymous*

Section 1

# Rhyming Words

## Word Family Lists

Family word lists present in the classroom are excellent tools for students to use during the development of early poetry writing skills. Use the word lists below to make rhyming family word charts or reproduce the word lists for the students to use.

| ip | ap | ag | at | in | ug |
|---|---|---|---|---|---|
| dip | cap | bag | bat | bin | bug |
| hip | gap | gag | cat | din | dug |
| nip | lap | hag | fat | fin | hug |
| rip | map | jag | hat | kin | jug |
| sip | nap | lag | mat | pin | lug |
| tip | rap | nag | pat | sin | mug |
| chip | sap | sag | rat | tin | pug |
| flip | tap | tag | vat | chin | tug |
| drip | yap | rag | chat | grin | rug |
| grip | zap | wag | flat | skin | drug |
| skip | clap | brag | gnat | spin | plug |
| slip | flap | drag | spat | thin | snug |
| snip | strap | flag | that | twin | smug |
| trip | trap | | | | |
| whip | wrap | | | | |

| ab | ad | am | it | ot | op |
|---|---|---|---|---|---|
| cab | bad | bam | bit | cot | cop |
| dab | cad | dam | fit | got | hop |
| gab | dad | ham | hit | hot | mop |
| jab | fad | jam | kit | lot | pop |
| tab | had | ram | lit | pot | top |
| crab | lad | tam | pit | tot | chop |
| drab | mad | clam | sit | rot | crop |
| grab | pad | cram | flit | blot | drop |
| flab | sad | sham | grit | knot | prop |
| scab | tad | slam | knit | plot | shop |
| slab | glad | tram | quit | trot | stop |
| stab | Brad | wham | slit | shot | |

Section 2

OTM-1874 • SSR1-74

# Word Family Lists

| et | og | ed | an | ew | id |
|----|----|----|----|----|----|
| bet | bog | bed | ban | dew | bid |
| fret | cog | fed | can | few | did |
| get | dog | led | fan | new | hid |
| jet | fog | red | man | pew | kid |
| let | frog | wed | pan | brew | lid |
| met | hog | bled | ran | chew | rid |
| net | jog | bred | tan | flew | grid |
| pet | log | fled | van | knew | skid |
| vet | smog | sled | scan | stew | squid |
| set | tog | sped | | | |
| wet | | | | | |

| ig | un | ut | en | ace | ade |
|----|----|----|----|-----|-----|
| big | bun | cut | den | face | blade |
| dig | fun | gut | hen | grace | fade |
| fig | gun | hut | men | lace | grade |
| jig | nun | nut | pen | mace | jade |
| pig | pun | rut | ten | pace | made |
| rig | run | glut | then | place | shade |
| wig | sun | shut | when | race | spade |
| brig | spun | strut | wren | space | trade |
| twig | stun | | | trace | wade |

| ake | ail | ing | ine | ill | ame |
|-----|-----|-----|-----|-----|-----|
| bake | bail | bring | dine | bill | blame |
| brake | fail | cling | fine | chill | came |
| cake | hail | fling | line | dill | dame |
| fake | jail | king | mine | drill | flame |
| flake | mail | ring | nine | fill | frame |
| lake | nail | sing | pine | grill | fame |
| make | pail | sling | shine | hill | game |
| rake | quail | spring | spine | ill | lame |
| sake | rail | sting | swine | kill | name |
| shake | sail | string | twine | mill | same |
| snake | snail | swing | vine | pill | shame |
| stake | tail | thing | whine | skill | tame |
| take | trail | wing | wine | spill | |
| wake | wail | wring | | till | |
| | | | | thrill | |
| | | | | will | |

Section 2

# Word Family Lists

| unk | ush | ick | ash | ank | ain |
|-----|-----|-----|-----|-----|-----|
| bunk | blush | brick | bash | bank | brain |
| chunk | brush | chick | brash | clank | chain |
| dunk | crush | click | cash | crank | drain |
| drunk | flush | kick | clash | drank | gain |
| hunk | gush | lick | crash | flank | grain |
| junk | hush | pick | dash | plank | main |
| punk | mush | quick | flash | prank | pain |
| shrunk | plush | sick | gash | sank | rain |
| skunk | rush | stick | hash | spank | sprain |
| spunk | slush | thick | mash | tank | stain |
| sunk | thrush | trick | rash | thank | strain |
| trunk | | wick | trash | yank | train |

| ate | ore | ack | ink | ell | est |
|-----|-----|-----|-----|-----|-----|
| crate | bore | back | blink | bell | best |
| date | core | black | drink | fell | chest |
| gate | more | crack | ink | sell | guest |
| hate | score | lack | link | shell | nest |
| late | shore | pack | mink | smell | pest |
| mate | snore | quack | pink | spell | rest |
| plate | sore | sack | shrink | swell | test |
| rate | store | stack | sink | tell | vest |
| skate | swore | tack | stink | well | west |
| slate | tore | track | think | yell | zest |
| state | wore | whack | wink | | |

| ave | ide | ice | amp | ump | ent |
|-----|-----|-----|-----|-----|-----|
| brave | bride | dice | camp | bump | bent |
| cave | glide | lice | champ | chump | dent |
| gave | guide | mice | clamp | clump | cent |
| grave | hide | nice | cramp | dump | lent |
| pave | pride | price | damp | hump | rent |
| rave | ride | rice | lamp | jump | sent |
| save | side | slice | ramp | slump | spent |
| shave | slide | spice | stamp | stump | lent |
| slave | tide | twice | tramp | thump | went |
| wave | wide | vice | | | |

Section 2

# Word Family Lists

| eam | eat | ee | eed | eep | oke |
|-----|-----|-----|-----|-----|-----|
| beam | beat | bee | bleed | cheep | broke |
| cream | cheat | fee | deed | creep | choke |
| dream | heat | flee | feed | deep | joke |
| gleam | meat | free | greed | keep | poke |
| scream | neat | knee | need | peep | smoke |
| seam | pleat | see | seed | sheep | spoke |
| steam | seat | tee | speed | sleep | stroke |
| stream | treat | three | tweed | steep | woke |
| team | wheat | tree | weed | weep | yoke |

| ose | ime | eet | and | ang | end |
|-----|-----|-----|-----|-----|-----|
| chose | chime | beet | band | bang | bend |
| close | crime | feet | brand | clang | blend |
| hose | dime | greet | grand | fang | lend |
| nose | grime | meet | hand | gang | mend |
| pose | lime | sweet | land | hang | send |
| rose | prime | sheet | sand | rang | spend |
| those | slime | sleet | stand | sang | tend |
| | time | street | strand | slang | vend |

| ess | ite | oat | | | |
|-----|-----|-----|-----|-----|-----|
| bless | bite | boat | | | |
| dress | kite | coat | | | |
| guess | site | goat | | | |
| less | spite | float | | | |
| mess | white | throat | | | |
| press | write | | | | |
| stress | | | | | |

Section 2

# Rhyming

Before children are exposed to the writing of formal poetry, time should be spent on listening for and learning rhyming words. Ear training is an essential skill that children need in order to distinguish sounds heard at the beginnings and endings of words.

Use any of the following suggestions to develop ear training:

1. Develop word family charts with your students. Review them regularly.

2. Use rhyming picture cards. Place them randomly on the chalkboard ledge. Have your students take turns finding pairs of rhyming words.

3. Hold up a pair of picture cards. Say their names. Ask your students if they rhyme.

4. Print rhyming words on cards. Place them on he chalkboard ledge. The students will pick out pairs of rhyming words.

5. Hold up a picture of a member of a word family for example "bed". Ask your students to brainstorm for words or things that rhyme with bed. They should give you words such as fed, led, red, wed, bled, bred, fled, sled, sped. Discuss their ending sounds.

6. Whenever you read poetry in the classroom discuss the rhyming words.

7. Use the ear training exercises provided in the book to strengthen listening skills and ear training.

# Ear Training Exercises

**Listening Exercise #1:**

I am going to say **two** words.  Please listen carefully.  Tell me if they **rhyme** or **do not** rhyme.

Say each group of words clearly.

1. hot, hat
2. cold, hold
3. flew, new
4. ship, shirt
5. bag, rag

6. beam, goat
7. rake, snake
8. rose, vine
9. bleed, weed
10. nail, nine

**Listening Exercise #2:**

I am going to say **three** words.  Please listen carefully.  Tell me if the words **rhyme** or **do not** rhyme.

Say each group of words clearly.

1. log, dog, jog
2. fig, fog, fan
3. fan, man, tan
4. mine, moan, mouse
5. hot, not, pot
6. crab, grab, cab
7. pop, pin, pan

8. sun, spun, bun
9. boat, boot, barn
10. cut, cop, cat
11. blink, wink, think
12. six, sack, two
13. big, door, pen
14. hop, mop, pop

Section 2

## Listening Exercise #3:

I am going to say three words.  Sometimes all **three** words rhyme.  Put your hand on your head if all **three** words rhyme.  Listen to the words carefully.

1. cop, drop, stop
2. in, it, is
3. pin, fin, fat
4. bet, pet, net
5. big, pig, wig
6. fine, line, dine
7. meat, seat, much
8. brave, cave, save
9. bell, bill, bowl
10. bank, clank, drank
11. mail, tail, mill
12. did, bib, lid
13. bump, clump, dump
14. lick, lack, luck
15. bend, sent, mend
16. hot, pot, cot

## Listening Exercise #4:

I am going to say four words.  If all **four** words rhyme raise your hand.  Listen carefully to the **four** words.

1. bog, dog, hog, jog
2. bun, fix, tan, gone
3. bin, fin, pin, tin
4. big, bag, bog, beg
5. pad, had, bad, sad
6. rag, rug, rig, way
7. map, mop, mill, miss
8. bell, spell, shell, swell
9. sack, sick, sock, suck
10. kill, mill, fill, pill
11. hunk, hack, hoot, hill
12. bump, mend, tell, fang
13. gush, mush, hush, flush
14. bash, hash, mash, cash
15. king, kite, kind, kill
16. sink, ink, blink, drink

## Listening Exercise #5:

I am going to say **three** words.  Listen carefully.  Tell me the names of the words that **rhyme**.

1. pin, pine, fine
2. sang, bang, soap
3. stamp, sand, land
4. lend, send, hide
5. best, bust, chest
6. hog, frog, hag
7. make, cake, coke
8. nut, not, cut
9. shop, hop, ship
10. smoke, smile, choke
11. flee, flew, new
12. sleep, sheet, peep
13. snail, snap, pail
14. rain, rail, pain
15. write, kite, keep
16. hat, ham, lamb

## Listening Exercise #6:

I am going to say **four** words.  Listen carefully.  Which words **rhyme**.

1. chime, dime, dumb, pine
2. crate, gate, late, wave
3. big, twig, nag, jump
4. whip, chin, slip, drip
5. shoot, shut, shack, boot
6. stop, shot, hop, pop
7. bit, fit, slit, shut
8. bed, bid, did, lid
9. dug, dig, bug, slug
10. bat, cab, hat, pin
11. dog, pot, got, doll
12. sip, nip, drip, hog
13. sleep, sheep, set, sea
14. see, bee, beat, three
15. mine, mice, rice, twice
16. spell, snail, pail, fill

# Word Family Rhyming

Rhyming words sound the same at the **end**.

Underline the words in each shape that belong to the word family.

**"ell"**

bell    ball

fall    fell

pack    bang

sell    sang    shell

smell    tall    dill    tell

will    well    went

**"ake"**

bike    beam

bake    cake

come    fake    lake

like    save    take

rake    ride    shake

**"ag"**

bun    tag    rag

run    nag    not

sag    tan    run

sap    rag    wag

van    car    flag

drag    did    big

**"ot"**

cat    let

got    go    cot

hat    pig    hot

lot    jam    pot

ten    shot    tan

trot    nut    log

Section 2

OTM-1874 • SSR1-74

| an |
| --- |
| **ban** |
| **can** |
| **fan** |
| **man** |
| **pan** |
| **ran** |
| **tan** |
| **van** |
| **scan** |

# Rhyme Time

Rhyming words sound the same at the **end**.

It is the beginning sound or sounds that change.

Rhyming words belong to families. Like the "an" word family on the little chart.

In each group of words below, **circle** the rhyming words.

| | | | | | | | | |
| --- | --- | --- | --- | --- | --- | --- | --- | --- |
| 1. | bed | den | fed | few | led | bug | tap | red |
| 2. | can | cap | man | mop | fan | fat | jam | ran |
| 3. | ten | tan | pen | red | men | rap | hen | den |
| 4. | ten | tan | pen | red | men | rap | hen | den |
| 5. | cap | cat | dug | hot | pot | pit | got | dog |
| 6. | bun | ban | run | hug | den | gun | sit | sun |
| 7. | dip | dad | lip | lit | sip | sad | nip | not |
| 8. | tell | tall | bell | bill | fell | fall | shell | spill |
| 9. | pan | pill | sink | bill | kill | kite | mill | mug |
| 10. | flag | fig | sag | bag | bog | tag | tug | jam |
| 11. | lick | luck | brick | bit | kick | wink | sick | sat |
| 12. | bump | lump | lack | dump | dug | hump | hit | bat |

Section 2

32

OTM-1874 • SSR1-74

# Rhyming Word Riddles

Can you solve the rhyming word riddles?

Use the words on the bear chart to help you.

Match the clues to the words.

| hen | black |
|-----|-------|
| ham | shell |
| hog | hat |
| red | bed |
| pop | jam |
| cat | shop |
| bell | pen |
| back | frog |

1. We belong to the "**ack**" word family. One is a color and one is part of your body. We are _____ and _____.

2. We belong to the "**ell**" word family. One of us rings and the other is part of a clam. We are _____ and _____.

3. We belong to the "**at**" word family. One word is an animal and one is something you wear. We are _____ and _____.

4. We belong to the "**op**" word family. One word is something to drink and the other is a place to buy things. We are _____ and _____.

5. We belong to the "**ed**" word family. One word is a color and the other is a place to sleep. We are _____ and _____.

6. We belong to the "**og**" word family. One word is a farm animal and the other lives in a pond. We are _____ and _____.

7. We belong to the "**am**" word family. We are both things to eat. One is sweet and one is a kind of meat. We are _____ and _____.

8. We belong to the "**en**" word family. One word is a farm bird and the other is something used for writing. The words are _____ and _____.

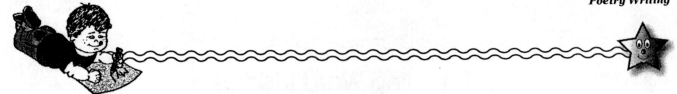

# Let's Begin to Write Poetry

Once your students have spent time listening to poetry, reading it and working with rhyming word families, it is time for them to work with rhyming couplets and familiar poetry.

A rhyming couplet in poetry is two lines that rhyme.

Write the following poem on chart paper. Print the missing words below it. Read the poem just as it is without the words. Have the students indicate where the missing words should go. Write them on the correct lines. Read the completed poem again.

**Example:**

### My Dad

My dad is a special _____.

He helps me whenever he _____.

He's always there to fix my _____.

And spends time doing things I _____.

bike     can     like     man

Use the following worksheets on pages 35 to 50 and have the students practice making rhyming couplets and simple poems.

# Let's Rhyme

Use the words written on the wall to complete the nursery rhyme.

Twinkle, twinkle, little _____,
How I wonder what you _____!
Up above the world so _____,
Like a diamond in the _____.

| | |
|---|---|
| sky | star |
| high | are |

---

Baa, baa, black sheep,
Have you any _____?
Yes, sir, yes, sir,
Three bags _____:

One for my master,
One for the _____,
But none for the little boy
Who lives down the _____.

| | |
|---|---|
| wool | full |
| lane | dame |

---

Hey diddle, _____,
The cat and the _____,
The cow jumped over the _____;
The little dog laughed
To see such sport,
And the dish ran away
With the _____.

| | |
|---|---|
| spoon | fiddle |
| moon | diddle |

---

Humpty Dumpty sat on a _____.
Humpty Dumpty had a great _____;
All the King's horses
And all the King's _____
Couldn't put Humpty together _____.

| | |
|---|---|
| again | wall |
| men | fall |

Section 2

# Nursery Rhyme Fun

Use the words in the shape to complete each nursery rhyme.

Little Jack _____
Sat in a _____ ,
Eating his Christmas _____ ;
He put in his _____ ,
And pulled out a _____ ,
And said,
"What a good boy am _____ ."

*Words in apple: corner, pie, thumb, plum, Horner, I*

Hickory, dickory, _____ ,
The mouse ran up the _____ ,
The clock struck _____ ,
The mouse ran _____ ,
Hickory, dickory _____ .

*Words in clock: dock, down, clock, one, dock*

Mary had a little lamb,
Its fleece was white as _____ ,
And everywhere that Mary went,
The lamb was sure to _____ .

He followed her to school one _____ ,
Which was against the _____ ,
It made the children laugh and _____ .
To see a lamb at _____ .

*Words in schoolhouse: go, play, day, rule, snow, school*

Section 2

# Family Rhymes

Use the words in the shape to complete each family rhyme.

## My Dad

My Dad is a special _____,

He helps me whenever he _____.

He's always there to fix my _____,

And spends time doing things I _____.

can

bike

like

man

## I Love My Mom

I love my Mom a whole _____,

When she makes my favorite _____.

I love my Mom when she _____,

And when she does special _____.

lunch

things

bunch

sings

## Brothers and Sisters

Brothers and sisters sometimes can _____,

Big pests who bother _____.

Other times their things they'll _____,

And then they become my _____.

lend

me

friend

be

# Winter Rhymes

Complete each winter rhyme with a word from the box.

Snowflakes falling
From the sky.
On my nose
And on my _____.

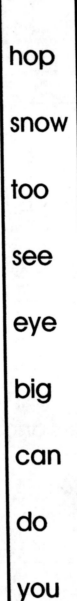

hat

hop

snow

too

see

eye

big

can

do

you

Snowman, snowman
Round and fat.
A funny nose
A big, black _____.

Making snowmen
Sliding too.
There are lots
Of things to _____.

Come on everyone
Out we go.
Let's have some fun
Out in the _____.

Section 2

# An Irish Rhyme

Can you complete the rhymes about the leprechauns?  Use the words in the pot of gold.

Five little leprechauns hiding behind the _____,
One jumped out and then there were _____.

Four little leprechauns sitting in a _____,
One fell out and then there were _____.

Three little leprechauns sleeping in a _____,
One got lost and then there were _____.

Two little leprechauns playing in the _____,
One disappeared and there was _____.

One little leprechaun was very _____,
He ran away with the pot of _____.

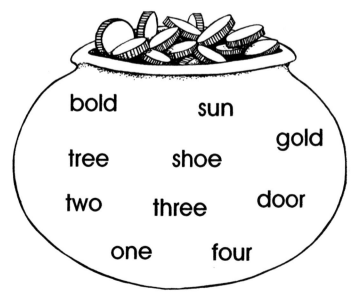

bold    sun

gold

tree    shoe

two    three    door

one    four

Section 2

# Rhyming Children

Can you complete the rhyme about the children? Use the words in the box.

Ten little children feeling just _____.
One got sick and then there were _____.

Nine little children swinging on a _____,
One stayed behind and then there were _____.

Eight little children one called _____,
He got lost and then there were _____.

Seven little children gathering _____,
One fell down and then there were _____.

Six little children very much _____,
One fell asleep and then there were _____.

Five little children hiding behind a _____,
One bumped his head and then there were _____.

Four little children happy as can _____,
One ran away and then there were _____.

Three little children all dressed in _____,
One got dirty and then there were _____.

Two little children playing in the _____,
One got dizzy and then there was _____.

One little child playing all _____,
She skipped away and then went back _____.

| |
|---|
| five |
| six |
| Kevin |
| sticks |
| fine |
| eight |
| door |
| be |
| blue |
| home |
| one |
| sun |
| alone |
| three |
| nine |
| gate |
| seven |
| four |
| two |
| alive |

Section 2

# Bug Rhymes

Complete each bug rhyme with the correct words found in the box under it.

Dragonfly, dragonfly
Over the pond you _____,
Like a helicopter
Going for a _____.

| tide | ride | hide | wide | glide | side |

Caterpillar, caterpillar
Fuzzy and _____.
You are the funniest sight
That I have ever _____.

| been | keen | seen | teen | queen | green |

Ladybug, ladybug!
Fly away _____!
Your house is on fire
And your children are all _____.

| home | comb | roam | alone | foam |

Butterfly so beautiful and _____.
You are a pretty _____!
As you quickly _____
So high up in the _____.

| light | fly | bright | shy | sight | sky |

Section 2

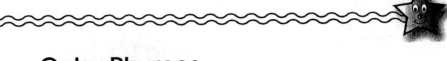

# Color Rhymes

Complete each color rhyme with a pair of rhyming words.

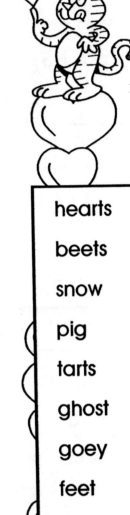

1. Red!  Red!
   What is red?
   Big Red _____ by my _____.

2. White!  White!
   What is white?
   Soft _____ we love to _____.

3. Pink!  Pink!
   What is pink?
   A farmer's _____, round and _____.

4. Red!  Red!
   What is red?
   Cinnamon _____ and cherry _____.

5. White!  White!
   What is white?
   A scary _____ sitting on a _____.

6. Pink!  Pink!
   What is pink?
   Bubble gum, _____ and _____.

hearts

beets

snow

pig

tarts

ghost

goey

feet

throw

post

big

chewy

Make up your own color rhyme using this pattern.

Section 2

OTM-1874 • SSR1-74

# Rhyming Couplets

A rhyming couplet is a two line poem that rhymes at the end.

Read this rhyming couplet.

> Have you ever seen a fish
> Swimming in a glass dish

Rhyming couplets are the easiest poems to write.

You can write a couplet about anything.

Examples:
    I have a cat named Pat,
    She likes to sleep on a mat.

    I love to go outside and play,
    On a bright, sunny day.

**Circle** the rhyming words in each couplet above.

Try to **write** a rhyming couplet using the rhyming words pig and jig.

_____

_____

Write a couplet about a frog.

_____

_____

Write a couplet about a mouse.

_____

_____

Section 3

# Mousey Rhymes

A **rhyming couplet** is a two line poem that rhymes at the end.

**Example:**   There's a hole in my house,
That is a home for a mouse.

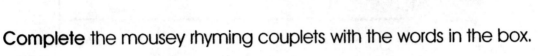

**Complete** the mousey rhyming couplets with the words in the box.

1. I knew the mouse was in the _____
   When I heard the loud _____ .

2. In the basement of my _____
   There lived a little gray _____ .

3. Mice like to eat _____
   And never have to say _____ .

4. In a quiet, dark _____
   Lived a mouse with whiskers on his _____ .

5. Mice will munch on _____
   And sometimes nibble on _____ .

6. I do not think that it would be _____
   To have my house invaded by _____ .

7. Mice like to play at _____
   When the cat is out of _____ .

| |
|---|
| night |
| house |
| place |
| cheese |
| roots |
| nice |
| boots |
| sight |
| face |
| mouse |
| snap |
| please |
| trap |
| mice |

**Section 3**

OTM-1874 • SSR1-74

# Vehicle Rhymes

A rhyming couplet is a two line poem that has rhyming endings.

Complete the rhyming couplets with the correct pair of rhyming words from the box.

1. Marie and David traveled _____ ,
   In the funny old yellow _____ .

2. Standing at the back of the _____ ,
   Stood a silly dressed up _____ .

3. Did you see that pretty pink _____ ,
   Traveling down the road with ten woolly _____ .

4. The soldier drove his big army _____ ,
   Up to the door of the new city _____ .

5. The children traveled to the _____ ,
   In a big red air _____ .

6. The captain of the old _____ ,
   Was known as Amos P. Billy _____ .

7. Driving the smelly garbage _____ ,
   Was a happy little yellow _____ .

8. Chug Chug was a big freight _____ ,
   He pulled his box cars in the snow, hail and _____ .

| | | | |
|---|---|---|---|
| train, rain | caboose, moose | car, far | truck, duck |
| moon, balloon | tank, bank | sheep, jeep | tugboat, Goat |

Section 3

# Rhyming Couplets
## Clinkety Clank's Rhymes

Clinkety Clank is a little bulldozer that loves to write rhyming couplets.

Complete each one with words from the box.

1. Have you ever seen a _____,
   Driving a great big _____.

2. The five little _____,
   Travel to school in a _____.

3. Look at Harry the big brown _____,
   Traveling in the red _____.

4. The soldier flew his _____,
   All the way in the _____.

5. The owl and the pussycat traveled _____,
   In the old, rickety _____.

6. The three little pigs went to the _____,
   In a colorful air _____.

7. Have you ever seen a _____,
   Driving a motor _____.

8. Oh look at the funny _____,
   Driving the red snow _____.

| |
|---|
| plow |
| balloon |
| plane |
| moose |
| jeep |
| car |
| ducks |
| moon |
| rain |
| goat |
| caboose |
| sheep |
| boat |
| far |
| truck |
| cow |

Section 3

# Rhyming Couplet Brainstorming

Remember, a rhyming couplet is a two line poem that sounds the same at the end.

On each shape below is a word.  Think of as many rhyming words as you can. **Write** the words in each shape.

Choose **two** of the rhyming words in each list and write your own rhyming couplet.

book

flag

jar

fall

Section 3

# Creative Couplets

Let's have fun with writing rhyming couplets.

Match the pictures below with a line to join the rhyming pairs.

Write rhyming couplets using each pair.

## Pictures

## Rhyming Couplets

1. _____

_____

2. _____

_____

3. _____

_____

4. _____

_____

Make up your own rhyming couplet.

_____

_____

Section 3

OTM-1874 • SSR1-74

# Writing Rhyming Couplets

**Look** at each picture below carefully.  **Think** of words that you could use before you start.

**Write** a rhyming couplet for each one.

49   Section 3   OTM-1874 • SSR1-74

# Writing Rhyming Couplets

Look at each picture below carefully. **Think** of words that you could use before you start.

**Write** a rhyming couplet for each one.

Section 3

# Two Word Poetry

Two word poems are just that - two words on each line.

You may have as many lines as you like but you are allowed only two words to each line.

These words may describe the topic's appearance, size, home, food and movement.

**Read** the two word poem below.

Example:

> ## Fish
>
> Sea creatures
> Gliding smoothly
> Silently moving
> In water

**Write** your own two word poem about one of the sea creatures in the box.

**Print** your poem on the shape card.

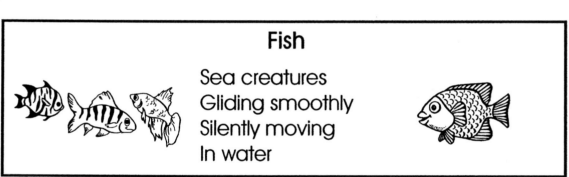

### Sea Creatures

| | | |
|---|---|---|
| octopus | lobster | dolphin |
| shark | clam | porpoise |
| whale | seahorse | squid |

Section 4

# My Two Word Poem

_____

_____

_____

_____

_____

_____

_____

_____

_____

Section 4

# Two Word Poetry

Two word poems are fun to write.

They do not rhyme.

You may have as many lines as you wish but you are allowed only two words to a line.

The words may describe the topic's appearance, size, home, food and the way it moves.

**Read** the two word poem below.

Example:

### Rabbits

Silent jumpers
Hopping quickly
Eating carrots
At night

Write your own two word poem about one of the forest animals in the box.

| Forest Animals | | |
|---|---|---|
| squirrels | skunks | foxes |
| bears | raccoons | porcupines |
| chipmunk | deer | beavers |

# Acrostic Poetry

Acrostic poetry is an enjoyable form of word play for young students. Each word or phrase of the poem begins with a letter in the topic.

It is important to read various examples of acrostic poetry to your students before they begin to write. Print some of the poems on chart paper. Be sure to print the first letter of each line a different color so the word will stand out. Display the poems around the classroom and share them with your students. The students could read them independently or in groups as a form of choral reading.

Below are some examples for you to use.

Cranberries
Ham
Raisins
Icing
Sweets
Turkey
Mincemeat
Apples
Sausages

See the snowman
Near the house
On the lawn
What a funny sight
Mittens on his head
Apple for his nose
Necktie for a sash

Lovely Leaves
Excite the world
Autumn is you time
For you to be Beautiful

Dashing through the forest
Expert, graceful, jumpers
Eating twigs and leaves
Resting in a safe glen

Section 5

# Acrostic Poetry

Tall and stately
Round you we gather
Excitedly waiting
Eager to see you glow

Frogs small and big
Roam all over the pond
On lily pads they sit
Gulping down fat flies
Sweetly croaking at night

Hamsters are soft
And very cuddly
Mounds of fluffy fur
Sound asleep
Their eyes closed
Each one curled into a ball
Rolled into a corner of the cage

Carefree and playful
Using his magic bow
Putting arrows of love
Into the hearts of people
Down on the earth below

Scattered everywhere
Even in sidewalk cracks
Eventually become plants
Downy and fluffy
Small and brown

Mighty Maple
Always standing stately
Providing us with cool shade
Lovely to see in the fall
Empty and bare in the winter

Section 5

# Writing Acrostic Poetry

Even though this form of poetry looks relatively easy for children to write, it does require careful thinking and selecting to create a sensible poem. With young students use only three-letter words.

Use the steps below to help you plan a lesson.

1.  Select a word that will interest your students. It could be a seasonal one, a special day, the name of a month or an animal's name.

2.  Discuss the letters in the word. On a chart make three columns. At the top of each column print the three letters. Then brainstorm for words that begin with each letter and describe the topic.

**Example:**

| D | O | G |
|---|---|---|
| dark brown | our pet | gobbles its food |
| digs holes | only likes me | gnaws bones |
| does tricks | opens doors | growls at noises |
| doesn't come | over eats | gets needles |
| does bark | on the bed | gives me licks |
| dirty paws | over the fence | goes in my bed |
| dashes around | obedient pet | goes for a ball |
| destroys toys | obeys me | gives us love |
| devoted pet | only a pup | guards our house |
| drinks water | | |

Section 5

# Writing Acrostic Poetry

**3.** Discuss the words and phrases on the chart. Have the children choose one phrase from each column, star each one.

**4.** Print the word vertically on a chart or the chalkboard. Print the phrases beside each letter.

**Example:**

> **D**oes tricks
>
> **O**ur pet
>
> **G**ives us love

**5.** Create other acrostic poems with the phrases. Have the children vote on the one they liked best.

**Examples:**

| | |
|---|---|
| **D**estroys toys | **D**ark brown |
| **O**nly a pup | **O**bedient pet |
| **G**ives me licks | **G**uards our house |
| | |
| **D**evoted pet | **D**oesn't come |
| **O**nly likes me | **O**pens doors |
| **G**oes in my bed | **G**obbles its food |
| | |
| **D**oes bark | **D**ashes around |
| **O**nly a pup | **O**nly a pup |
| **G**oes for a ball | **G**ets needles |

**6.** The children could copy one of the acrostic poems and illustrate it.

Section 5

# About Acrostics

Acrostic poems are written vertically.  Just think of a word and write it down like this:

> Crispy, crunchy
> Oven baked
> Oatmeal raisin
> Kids eat them
> Indoors and outdoors
> Eaten quickly
> Snacktime treat

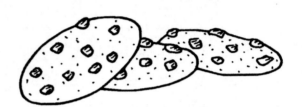

Acrostic poems do not rhyme.  You may use as many words as you like in each line.

Write your own acrostic poem about something you like to eat.

**Choose** a word from the poetry box and **write** your own acrostic poem.

sandwich
cake
apples
candy
hot dogs
soda pop
soup
ice cream
jello
pudding
milk
pizza

_____
_____
_____
_____
_____
_____
_____
_____

Section 5

# What is an Acrostic Poem?

An acrostic poem is one where the name or word is written vertically.

Example:

Shiny silver blades
Keep us on our feet
A pair of boots
Tied  with laces
Easily glide on ice
Some are white, some are black

Beside each letter is a group of words or a sentence that talks about the topic.

The first word must begin with the letter.

**Choose** one of the winter words found in the mitten.

**Write** an acrostic poem about it.

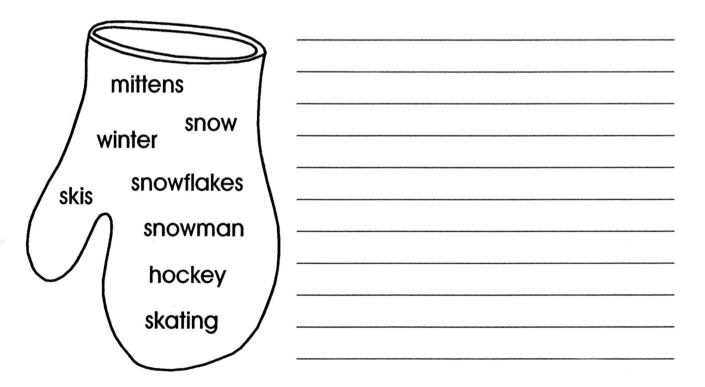

mittens
snow
winter
snowflakes
skis
snowman
hockey
skating

Section 5

OTM-1874 • SSR1-74

# Write a Character Acrostic

Write an acrostic poem about your favorite storybook character.

Here is one about Curious George

Example:

> George is a funny monkey
> Everyone likes him
> One day he played with the phone
> Ring, ring, ring it went
> George called the fire station
> Every fireman came to his house

**Choose** your favorite storybook character.

**Print** the name vertically on the lines below.

_____

_____

_____

_____

_____

_____

_____

_____

_____

_____

_____

_____

Section 5

# Writing a Vehicle Acrostic

Read the acrostic poem about "Airplanes".

An acrostic poem does not rhyme.

Remember:

- letters of the word are written vertically

- words and phrases must talk about the topic.

Airplanes fly way up high
I can see them flying by
Riding above fluffy clouds
Popular way to travel places
Large and small land at the airport
All day long
Noisy vehicles roaring loudly
Engines checked over carefully
So we will have a safe trip

Choose **one** of the words from the box.
Write an **acrostic** poem on the lines below. **Illustrate** the vehicle.

| car | train | helicopter | bicycle |
| van | truck | space shuttle | bus |
| jeep | canoe | sail boat | street car |

Picture

_____

_____

_____

_____

_____

_____

_____

# Finish the Limericks

A **limerick** is a funny poem with **five** lines.

Use the words in the box under it to finish each limerick.  Write the words on the lines.

1. There once was a sunfish named _____
   Who was always very, very _____
   She saw a little _____
   Who began to _____
   Then she began to act _____!

   | lazy | worm | Daisy | crazy | squirm |

2. There once was a bunny called _____
   Who thought that he was very _____
   All the day _____
   He sang silly _____
   Trying to make himself some _____

   | songs | Sunny | long | money | funny |

3. There once was a squid named _____
   Who during the day often _____
   When a fish swam _____
   Out he would _____
   And I guess I'll never know why he _____!

   | hid | fly | did | by | Sid |

Choose the limerick you liked the best.

Illustrate the character in it.

Section 6

# Finish the Limericks

Remember limericks are **funny** poems with **five** lines.

Use the words in the box under each limerick to finish it. Write the missing words on the lines.

1. There once was a unicorn named _____
   Who sang in the unicorn _____
   When he sang _____
   His horn grew so _____
   That he couldn't walk through the _____.

   | songs | Horace | forest | long | chorus |

2. There once was a leprechaun named _____
   Who loved to eat foods that were _____
   He ate strawberries for _____
   And cherries by the _____
   Till he was so sick he went to _____.

   | red | lunch | bed | Fred | bunch |

3. There once was a witch named _____
   Who had a black cat named _____
   When the moon was in _____
   One spooky Halloween _____
   Away they both flew looking _____.

   | night | Tilly | sight | silly | Billy |

Chose the limerick that you like the best.

Copy it neatly in your best printing.

Section 6

# Writing a Limerick

A **limerick** is a poem with five lines.
The rhyming pattern is a - a - b - b - a. It is usually a funny poem.

> There once was a cat named Kitty.
> Who lived on the streets of a city
> She had no home
> All over she roamed
> She was dirty and not very pretty.

Look at lines one, two and five.
What do the last words do? _____

Read lines three and four.
What do the last words do? _____

Let's try to write our own limerick.

Think of a funny thing that has happened to an animal.

Who was the animal? _____

Where did the funny thing take place? _____

What happened? _____
_____

How did it end? _____
_____

Begin your limerick with "There once was a" or 'There was a"

**Line One:** Choose your beginning and finish it.

_____

_____

Section 6

# Writing a Limerick

**Line Two:**

Line Two of a limerick has the same beat as the first line. It tells you more about the animal in the first line. The ends of line one and two rhyme.

Write Line Two here:

_____

**Lines Three and Four:**

Lines Three and Four have a different beat and different rhyming words at the end. These lines tell more about the animal or something funny.

Write Lines Three and Four on the lines below.

_____

_____

**Line Five:**

The last line of the limerick has the same beat as Lines One and Two. The last word of this line rhymes with the words at the end of lines one and two.

Write Line Five on the line below.

_____

Now write your limerick poem on the lines in the box below.

_____
_____
_____
_____
_____

Section 6

# Writing a Vehicle Limerick

A **limerick** is a funny poem made of five lines.

Lines one, two and five rhyme at the end and have the same beat.

They are longer than lines three and four.

Lines three and four rhyme too.

Read the following limerick.

> There once was a sad car named Rusty,
> Who sat in a barn getting dusty.
> Once he was new,
> Over roads he flew
> Now he's dingy and smells very musty.

Choose one of the beginning sentences and write a limerick. Print it in the truck shape card.

1. There once was a helicopter named Harry,

2. There once was a train called Clickety - Clack,

3. There once was a jet named Zoom - Zoom,

4. There once was a wild car named Bang - Bang,

5. There once was a little tugboat named Toot - Toot,

6. There once was a bus named Bumpity - Bump,

My Vehicle Limerick

Section 6

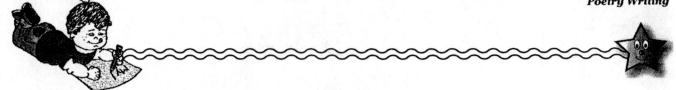

# Haiku

Younger students will find it difficult to write an actual seventeen syllable haiku. They can show and express a feeling within a one sentence format.

Here is a simple pattern to follow.

- Where it takes place    –    On the banks of a river
- What is happening    –    A lonely deer drinks
- When it occurs    –    Each summer evening

A traditional Haiku poem consists of seventeen syllables written in three lines.

Line One    –    5 syllables

Line Two    –    7 syllables

Line Three    –    5 syllables

**Haiku** poems usually refer to something in nature. They share a moment of beauty which makes one think about the subject. The important part of a haiku is the thought, then think about changing the syllable count.

**Examples:**

In the flowerbed
Flitting among the flowers
The bee sips the nector

In the quaint garden
The lovely daffodils swayed
in the gentle breeze

       OTM-1874 • SSR1-74

# Writing a Haiku

Young students require assistance during the writing of a haiku.

Use the steps below to help you plan a lesson.

1. Select a topic pertaining to nature. Use a picture showing a seasonal scene. Discuss the picture with your students.

2. Brainstorm and write lists of words and phrases on the chalkboard or on a chart that tell "where" the action is occurring. This list is labeled "where".

3. Brainstorm and create lists of words and phrases that tell "what" is happening. Record them on another chart labeled "what".

4. Brainstorm and write words and phrases that tell "when" the event is taking place. Record them on a chart labeled "when".

**Example:**

| **Where** | **What** | **When** |
|---|---|---|
| In the forest | Leaves are falling | During the fall |
| In a woodlot | Pretty trees stand | In October |
| In the woods | Beautiful trees are seen | During autumn days |
| In a shady glade | Colorful leaves fall | Autumn time |
| In the valley | Animals are busy | Before winter comes |
| Near a brook | Birds are flying south | During the autumn |
| In the mountains | Squirrels collect nuts | In late autumn |
| By a pond | Bears eat berries | On autumn days |

# Writing a Haiku

**5.** Have the children read each chart out loud. They are to choose a "where", a "what", and a "when" phrase to complete the idea.

**6.** Record their choices on a chart. Have them read their haiku. You may have to do this several times before they create a good one. After you have several created, have the students select the one that they like the best.

Possible Haiku Poetry:

| | |
|---|---|
| In the forest<br>Leaves are falling<br>During the fall | In their woods<br>Animals are busy<br>Before winter comes |
| In a woodlot<br>Beautiful trees are seen<br>During the autumn | In a shady glade<br>Squirrels collect nuts<br>During autumn days |
| In the mountains<br>Bears eat berries<br>Before winter comes | In the valley<br>Birds are flying south<br>On autumn days |

**7.** The students will copy the chosen haiku and illustrate it.

**8.** This activity should be repeated many times before your students write one on their own.

Section 7

# Haiku Matching

Cut out each haiku poem.  Glue it under the picture it describes.

| | |
|---|---|
| | |
| | |

| | |
|---|---|
| On a big, green lily pad<br>Sat a fat, spotted bullfrog<br>Sunning himself in the sun | In the old, oak tree<br>A horned owl sat<br>In the dark of the night |
| In the beautiful web<br>Sat a big, fat spider<br>Waiting for its dinner | In a pretty flower garden<br>A butterfly flits about<br>When the sun is bright |

# Reading Haiku Poetry

Read each haiku poem carefully.  In the box beside the poem draw a picture of it.

| | |
|---|---|
| 1.  Up in the sky so high<br><br>Geese are quickly flying<br><br>In the late fall | |
| 2.  In my dad's garden<br><br>A caterpillar spins a cocoon<br><br>On a cool autumn day | |
| 3.  In a cage with bars<br><br>The lion walks about<br><br>All day long | |
| 4.  On a nest in the barn<br><br>Sits a little brown hen<br><br>Waiting for morning | |

# Writing a Haiku

On the page you will find some pictures and phrases.  Write a haiku using the phrases about each picture.

Print the phrases under the correct picture.

Remember where, what, and when.

_____
Where

_____
What

_____
When

_____
Where

_____
What

_____
When

On a mild winter's day

Catching insects at night

Where there is no light

Where the snow is not deep

The bat flies about

The animals meet at the tree

OTM-1874 • SSR1-74

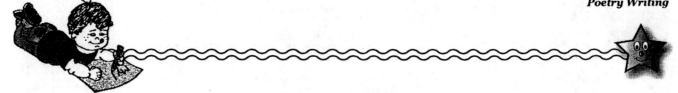

# What is a Cinquain

The best type of cinquain to teach young students to write is a Word Count Cinquain.  It relies on a word count rather than a syllable count.

## Word Count Cinquain Pattern

Line 1  –  one word *(title)*

Line 2  –  two words *(describes the title)*

Line 3  –  three words *(describes an action)*

Line 4  –  four words *(describes a feeling)*

Line 5  –  one word *(refers to the title)*

**Examples:**

Wolf
Swift, ferocious
Hunts for food
Running with the pack
Hunter

Kitten
Soft, furry
Chasing its tail
Loving, happy, purring pet
Cuddly

Section 8

# Cinquain Poetry

Cinquain poetry writing requires a great deal of listening and group writing before young children are able to create poems independently. Cinquains should be read to the students frequently before writing takes place. The cinquains provided will help you to get started. Write them on charts and group read them with the students.

George
Curious monkey
He's always bad
Always getting into trouble
Ape

Squirrel
Frisky, quick
Gathering many nuts
Chattering noisily at me
Saucy

Webs
Delicate nests
Spun by spiders
Deadly traps for insects
Homes

Lion
Scary, large
Leaps, pounces, springs
Surprises his prey easily
Beast

Droofus
Scaly brute
Flying, swooping, circling
Kind, gentle looking monster
Dragon

Snow
White fluff
Floating and falling
Fun to play in
Crystals

Robins
Spring Warblers
Flying, swooping, singing
Like to build nests
Birds

Pumpkins
Orange balls
Changing on Halloween
You light our way
Lanterns

Section 8

OTM-1874 • SSR1-74

# Writing a Cinquain

Young students require a great deal of assistance and practice to prepare them for cinquain writing.  Use the ideas below to help you in your lesson planning.

1. Select a topic in which your are interested.  Print the title on the chalkboard.

2. Have the following charts prepared.

    **a)** Words That Describe the Title

    **b)** Three Word Action Phrases

    **c)** Four Word Feeling Phrases

    **d)** Words That Refer to the Title

3. Brainstorm and make a list of words that describe the title.  Print the words on number one chart.

4. Brainstorm and make a list of three-word phrases that describe an action relating to the topic.  Record the three-word phrases on chart number two.

5. Brainstorm and make a list of four-word phrases that describe a feeling experienced by or about the topic.  Record the four-word phrases on chart number three.

6. Brainstorm and make a list of words that refer to the title.  Print these words on chart number four.

7. The class decides on a word or phrase for each line of the cinquain.

Example of Brainstorming Charts.

## Topic : Bunny

| **1. Words That Describe the Title** | **2. Three Word Action Phrases** |
|---|---|
| Furry coat | Loves eating carrots |
| Soft fur | Hops all around |
| Fluffy tail | Listens for danger |
| White fur | Wriggles its nose |
| Pink nose | Looking for food |
| Long whiskers | Hops and stops |
| Twitching ears | Hides under bushes |
| Wiggly nose | Stands very still |
| Big teeth | Watches for danger |
| Long ears | Sniffs the grass |
| Big eyes | Nibbles little branches |

| **3. Four Word Feeling Phrases** | **4. Words That Refer to Title** |
|---|---|
| Afraid of big owl | Pet |
| Scared of Mr. Fox | Animal |
| Feels safe in holes | Baby |
| Knows when there's danger | Rabbit |
| Hides from the fox | Mammal |
| Always wants to eat | Thumper |
| Stays near its mother | |
| Afraid of big shadows | |
| Runs from loud noises | |

Section 8

# Writing a Cinquain

Sample Cinquain:

> Bunny
>
> Long ears
>
> Listening for dangers
>
> Afraid of Mr. Owl
>
> Baby

Other Possible Cinquains.

| | |
|---|---|
| Bunny<br>Soft fur<br>Wriggles its nose<br>Runs from loud noises<br>Thumper | Bunny<br>Big eyes<br>Looking for food<br>Always wants to eat<br>Mammal |
| Bunny<br>Big teeth<br>Nibbles little branches<br>Stays near its mother<br>Baby | Bunny<br>Twitching ears<br>Watches for danger<br>Afraid of big shadows<br>Animal |

# An Autumn Cinquain

In the autumn the leaves are beautiful colors.

Write a cinquain about "**leaves**" in the bag.

_____
Topic

_____ _____
Two words that describe the topic

_____ _____ _____
Three word action phrase

_____ _____ _____ _____
Four word feeling phrase

_____
A word that talks about the title

Section 8

# A Winter Cinquain

In the winter snow is soft and fluffy.

Write a cinquain about the "**snow**" in winter.

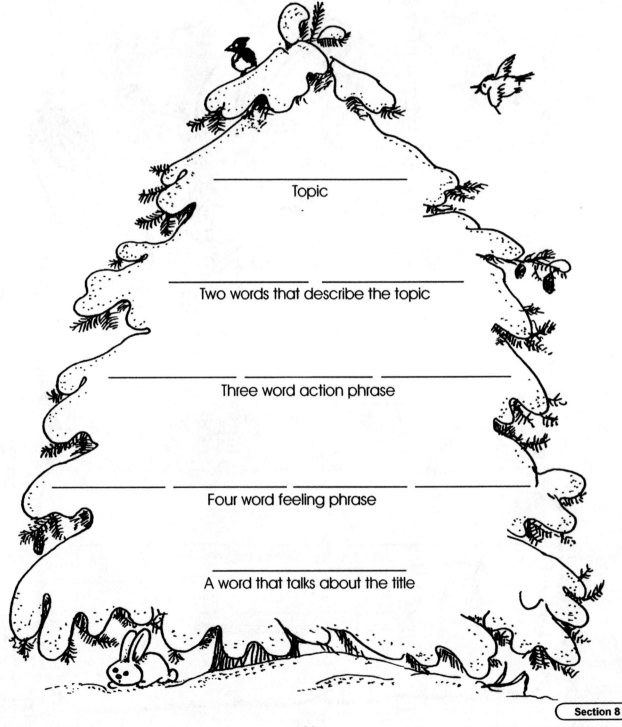

_____
Topic

_____ _____
Two words that describe the topic

_____ _____ _____
Three word action phrase

_____ _____ _____ _____
Four word feeling phrase

_____
A word that talks about the title

Section 8

OTM-1874 • SSR1-74

# Publication Listing

# Publication Listing

| Code # | Title and Grade |
|---|---|
| SSN1-100 | Indian in the Cupboard NS Gr. 4-6 |
| SSPC-05 | Insects B/W Pictures |
| SSPC-10 | Inuit B/W Pictures |
| SSJ1-10 | Inuit Community Gr. 3-4 |
| SSN1-85 | Ira Sleeps Over NS Gr. 1-3 |
| SSN1-93 | Iron Man NS Gr. 4-6 |
| SSN1-193 | Island of the Blue Dolphins NS 4-6 |
| SSB1-11 | It's a Dogs World Gr. 2-3 |
| SSM1-05 | It's a Marshmallow World Gr. 3 |
| SSK1-05 | It's About Time Gr. 2-4 |
| SSC1-41 | It's Christmas Time Gr. 3 |
| SSH1-04 | It's Circus Time Gr. 1 |
| SSC1-43 | It's Groundhog Day Gr. 3 |
| SSB1-75 | It's Maple Syrup Time Gr. 2-4 |
| SSC1-40 | It's Trick or Treat Time Gr. 2 |
| SSN1-65 | James & The Giant Peach NS 4-6 |
| SSN1-106 | Jane Eyre NS Gr. 7-8 |
| SSPC-25 | Japan B/W Pictures |
| SSA1-06 | Japan Gr. 5-8 |
| SSC1-05 | Joy of Christmas Gr. 2 |
| SSN1-161 | Julie of the Wolves NS Gr. 7-8 |
| SSB1-81 | Jungles Gr. 2-3 |
| SSE1-02 | Junior Music for Fall Gr. 4-6 |
| SSE1-05 | Junior Music for Spring Gr. 4-6 |
| SSE1-06 | Junior Music for Winter Gr. 4-6 |
| SSN1-151 | Kate NS Gr. 4-6 |
| SSN1-95 | Kidnapped in the Yukon NS Gr. 4-6 |
| SSN1-140 | Kids at Bailey School Gr. 2-4 |
| SSN1-176 | King of the Wind NS Gr. 4-6 |
| SSF1-29 | Klondike Gold Rush Gr. 4-6 |
| SSF1-33 | Labour Movement in Canada Gr. 7-8 |
| SSN1-152 | Lamplighter NS Gr. 4-6 |
| SSB1-98 | Learning About Dinosaurs Gr. 3 |
| SSN1-38 | Learning About Giants Gr. 4-6 |
| SSK1-22 | Learning About Measurement Gr. 1-3 |
| SSB1-46 | Learning About Mice Gr. 3-5 |
| SSK1-09 | Learning About Money CDN Gr. 1-3 |
| SSK1-19 | Learning About Money USA Gr. 1-3 |
| SSK1-23 | Learning About Numbers Gr. 1-3 |
| SSB1-69 | Learning About Rocks & Soils Gr. 2-3 |
| SSK1-08 | Learning About Shapes Gr. 1-3 |
| SSB1-100 | Learning About Simple Machines 1-3 |
| SSK1-04 | Learning About the Calendar Gr. 2-3 |
| SSK1-10 | Learning About Time Gr. 1-3 |
| SSH1-17 | Learning About Transportation Gr. 1 |
| SSB1-02 | Leaves Gr. 2-3 |
| SSN1-50 | Legends Gr. 4-6 |
| SSC1-27 | Lest We Forget Gr. 4-6 |
| SSJ1-13 | Let's Look at Canada Gr. 4-6 |
| SSJ1-16 | Let's Visit Alberta Gr. 2-4 |
| SSJ1-15 | Let's Visit British Columbia Gr. 2-4 |
| SSJ1-03 | Let's Visit Canada Gr. 3 |
| SSJ1-18 | Let's Visit Manitoba Gr. 2-4 |
| SSJ1-21 | Let's Visit New Brunswick Gr. 2-4 |
| SSJ1-27 | Let's Visit NFLD & Labrador Gr. 2-4 |
| SSJ1-30 | Let's Visit North West Terr. Gr. 2-4 |
| SSJ1-20 | Let's Visit Nova Scotia Gr. 2-4 |
| SSJ1-34 | Let's Visit Nunavut Gr. 2-4 |
| SSJ1-17 | Let's Visit Ontario Gr. 2-4 |
| SSQ1-08 | Let's Visit Ottawa Big Book Pkg 1-3 |
| SSJ1-19 | Let's Visit PEI Gr. 2-4 |
| SSJ1-31 | Let's Visit Québec Gr. 2-4 |
| SSJ1-14 | Let's Visit Saskatchewan Gr. 2-4 |
| SSJ1-28 | Let's Visit Yukon Gr. 2-4 |
| SSN1-130 | Life & Adv. of Santa Claus NS 7-8 |
| SSB1-10 | Life in a Pond Gr. 3-4 |
| SSF1-30 | Life in the Middle Ages Gr. 7-8 |
| SSB1-103 | Light & Sound Gr. 4-6 |
| SSN1-219 | Light in the Forest NS Gr. 7-8 |
| SSN1-121 | Light on Hogback Hill NS Gr. 4-6 |
| SSN1-46 | Lion, Witch & the Wardrobe NS 4-6 |
| SSR1-51 | Literature Response Forms Gr. 1-3 |
| SSR1-52 | Literature Response Forms Gr. 4-6 |
| SSN1-28 | Little House Big Woods NS 4-6 |
| SSN1-233 | Little House on the Prairie NS 4-6 |
| SSN1-111 | Little Women NS Gr. 7-8 |
| SSN1-115 | Live from the Fifth Grade NS 4-6 |
| SSN1-141 | Look Through My Window NS 4-6 |
| SSN1-112 | Look! Visual Discrimination Gr. P-1 |
| SSN1-61 | Lost & Found NS Gr. 4-6 |
| SSN1-109 | Lost in the Barrens NS Gr. 7-8 |
| SSJ1-08 | Lumbering Community Gr. 3-4 |
| SSN1-167 | Magic School Bus Gr. 1-3 |
| SSN1-247 | Magic Treehouse Gr. 1-3 |
| SSB1-78 | Magnets Gr. 3-5 |
| SSD1-03 | Making Sense of Our Senses K-1 |
| SSN1-146 | Mama's Going to Buy You a NS 4-6 |
| SSB1-94 | Mammals Gr. 1 |
| SSB1-95 | Mammals Gr. 2 |
| SSB1-96 | Mammals Gr. 3 |
| SSB1-97 | Mammals Gr. 5-6 |
| SSN1-160 | Maniac Magee NS Gr. 4-6 |
| SSA1-19 | Mapping Activities & Outlines! 4-8 |
| SSA1-17 | Mapping Skills Gr. 1-3 |
| SSA1-07 | Mapping Skills Gr. 4-6 |
| SST1-10A | March Gr. JK/SK |
| SST1-10B | March Gr. 1 |
| SST1-10C | March Gr. 2-3 |
| SSB1-57 | Marvellous Marsupials Gr. 4-6 |
| SSK1-01 | Math Signs & Symbols Gr. 1-3 |
| SSB1-116 | Matter & Materials Gr. 1-3 |
| SSB1-117 | Matter & Materials Gr. 4-6 |
| SSH1-03 | Me, I'm Special! Gr. P-1 |
| SSK1-16 | Measurement Gr. 4-8 |
| SSC1-02 | Medieval Christmas Gr. 4-6 |
| SSPC-09 | Medieval Life B/W Pictures |
| SSC1-07 | Merry Christmas Gr. P-K |
| SSK1-15 | Metric Measurement Gr. 4-8 |
| SSN1-13 | Mice in Literature Gr. 3-5 |
| SSB1-70 | Microscopy Gr. 4-6 |
| SSN1-180 | Midnight Fox NS Gr. 4-6 |
| SSN1-243 | Midwife's Apprentice NS Gr. 4-6 |
| SSJ1-07 | Mining Community Gr. 3-4 |
| SSK1-17 | Money Talks – Cdn Gr. 3-6 |
| SSK1-18 | Money Talks – USA Gr. 3-6 |
| SSB1-56 | Monkeys & Apes Gr. 4-6 |
| SSN1-43 | Monkeys in Literature Gr. 2-4 |
| SSN1-54 | Monster Mania Gr. 4-6 |
| SSN1-97 | Mouse & the Motorcycle NS 4-6 |
| SSN1-94 | Mr. Poppers Penguins NS Gr. 4-6 |
| SSN1-201 | Mrs. Frisby & Rats NS Gr. 4-6 |
| SSR1-13 | Milti-Level Spelling Program Gr. 3-6 |
| SSR1-26 | Multi-Level Spelling USA Gr. 3-6 |
| SSK1-31 | Addition & Subtraction Drills 1-3 |
| SSK1-32 | Multiplication & Division Drills 4-6 |
| SSK1-30 | Multiplication Drills Gr. 4-6 |
| SSA1-14 | My Country! The USA! Gr. 2-4 |
| SSN1-186 | My Side of the Mountain NS 7-8 |
| SSN1-58 | Mysteries, Monsters & Magic Gr. 6-8 |
| SSN1-37 | Mystery at Blackrock Island NS 7-8 |
| SSN1-80 | Mystery House NS 4-6 |
| SSN1-157 | Nate the Great & Sticky Case NS 1-3 |
| SSF1-23 | Native People of North America 4-6 |
| SSF1-25 | New France Part 1 Gr. 7-8 |
| SSF1-27 | New France Part 2 Gr. 7-8 |
| SSA1-10 | New Zealand Gr. 4-8 |
| SSN1-51 | Newspapers Gr. 5-8 |
| SSN1-47 | No Word for Goodbye NS Gr. 7-8 |
| SSPC-03 | North American Animals B/W Pictures |
| SSF1-22 | North American Natives Gr. 2-4 |
| SSN1-75 | Novel Ideas Gr. 4-6 |
| SST1-06A | November JK/SK |
| SST1-06B | November Gr. 1 |
| SST1-06C | November Gr. 2-3 |
| SSN1-244 | Number the Stars NS Gr. 4-6 |
| SSY1-03 | Numeration Gr. 1-3 |
| SSPC-14 | Nursery Rhymes B/W Pictures |
| SSN1-12 | Nursery Rhymes Gr. P-1 |
| SSN1-59 | On the Banks of Plum Creek NS 4-6 |
| SSN1-220 | One in Middle Green Kangaroo NS 1-3 |
| SSN1-145 | One to Grow On NS Gr. 4-6 |
| SSB1-27 | Opossums Gr. 3-5 |
| SSJ1-23 | Ottawa Gr. 7-9 |
| SSJ1-39 | Our Canadian Governments Gr. 5-8 |
| SSF1-14 | Our Global Heritage Gr. 4-6 |
| SSH1-12 | Our Neighbourhoods Gr. 4-6 |
| SSB1-72 | Our Trash Gr. 2-3 |
| SSB1-51 | Our Universe Gr. 5-8 |
| SSB1-86 | Outer Space Gr. 1-2 |
| SSA1-18 | Outline Maps of the World Gr. 1-8 |
| SSB1-67 | Owls Gr. 4-6 |
| SSN1-31 | Owls in the Family NS Gr. 4-6 |
| SSL1-02 | Oxbridge Owl & The Library Gr. 4-6 |
| SSB1-71 | Pandas, Polar & Penguins Gr. 4-6 |
| SSN1-52 | Paperbag Princess NS Gr. 1-3 |
| SSR1-11 | Passion of Jesus: A Play Gr. 7-8 |
| SSA1-12 | Passport to Adventure Gr. 4-5 |
| SSR1-06 | Passport to Adventure Gr. 7-8 |
| SSR1-04 | Personal Spelling Dictionary Gr. 2-5 |
| SSPC-29 | Pets B/W Pictures |
| SSE1-03 | Phantom of the Opera Gr. 7-9 |
| SSN1-171 | Phoebe Gilman Author Study Gr. 2-3 |
| SSY1-06 | Phonics Gr. 1-3 |
| SSN1-237 | Pierre Berton Author Study Gr. 7-8 |
| SSN1-179 | Pigman NS Gr. 7-8 |
| SSN1-48 | Pigs in Literature Gr. 2-4 |
| SSN1-99 | Pinballs NS Gr. 4-6 |
| SSN1-60 | Pippi Longstocking NS Gr. 4-6 |
| SSF1-12 | Pirates Gr. 4-6 |
| SSK1-13 | Place Value Gr. 4-6 |
| SSB1-77 | Planets Gr. 3-6 |
| SSR1-74 | Poetry Prompts Gr. 1-3 |
| SSR1-75 | Poetry Prompts Gr. 4-6 |
| SSB1-66 | Popcorn Fun Gr. 2-3 |
| SSB1-20 | Porcupines Gr. 3-5 |
| SSR1-55 | Practice Manuscript Gr. Pk-2 |
| SSR1-56 | Practice Cursive Gr. 2-4 |
| SSF1-24 | Prehistoric Times Gr. 4-6 |
| SSE1-01 | Primary Music for Fall Gr. 1-3 |
| SSE1-04 | Primary Music for Spring Gr. 1-3 |
| SSE1-07 | Primary Music for Winter Gr. 1-3 |
| SSJ1-47 | Prime Ministers of Canada Gr. 4-8 |
| SSK1-20 | Probability & Inheritance Gr. 7-10 |
| SSN1-49 | Question of Loyalty NS Gr. 7-8 |
| SSN1-26 | Rabbits in Literature Gr. 2-4 |
| SSB1-17 | Raccoons Gr. 3-5 |
| SSN1-207 | Radio Fifth Grade NS Gr. 4-6 |
| SSB1-52 | Rainbow of Colours Gr. 4-6 |
| SSN1-144 | Ramona Quimby Age 8 NS 4-6 |
| SSJ1-09 | Ranching Community Gr. 3-4 |
| SSY1-08 | Reading for Meaning Gr. 1-3 |
| SSN1-165 | Reading Response Forms Gr. 1-3 |
| SSN1-239 | Reading Response Forms Gr. 4-6 |
| SSN1-234 | Reading with Arthur Gr. 1-3 |
| SSN1-249 | Reading with Canadian Authors 1-3 |
| SSN1-200 | Reading with Curious George Gr. 2-4 |
| SSN1-230 | Reading with Eric Carle Gr. 1-3 |
| SSN1-251 | Reading with Kenneth Oppel Gr. 4-6 |
| SSN1-127 | Reading with Mercer Mayer Gr. 1-2 |
| SSN1-07 | Reading with Motley Crew Gr. 2-3 |
| SSN1-142 | Reading with Robert Munsch 1-3 |
| SSN1-06 | Reading with the Super Sleuths 4-6 |
| SSN1-08 | Reading with the Ziggles Gr. 1 |
| SST1-11A | Red Gr. JK/SK |
| SSN1-147 | Refuge NS Gr. 7-8 |
| SSC1-44 | Remembrance Day Gr. 1-3 |
| SSPC-23 | Reptiles B/W Pictures |
| SSB1-42 | Reptiles Gr. 4-6 |
| SSN1-110 | Return of the Indian NS Gr. 4-6 |
| SSN1-225 | River NS Gr. 7-8 |
| SSE1-08 | Robert Schuman, Composer Gr. 6-9 |
| SSN1-83 | Robot Alert NS Gr. 4-6 |
| SSB1-65 | Rocks & Minerals Gr. 4-6 |
| SSN1-149 | Romeo & Juliet NS Gr. 7-8 |
| SSB1-88 | Romping Reindeer Gr. K-3 |
| SSN1-21 | Rumplestiltskin NS Gr. 1-3 |
| SSN1-153 | Runaway Ralph NS Gr. 4-6 |
| SSN1-103 | Sadako & 1000 Paper Cranes NS 4-6 |
| SSD1-04 | Safety Gr. 2-4 |
| SSN1-42 | Sarah Plain & Tall NS Gr. 4-6 |
| SSC1-34 | School in September Gr. 4-6 |
| SSPC-01 | Sea Creatures B/W Pictures |
| SSB1-79 | Sea Creatures Gr. 1-3 |
| SSN1-64 | Secret Garden NS Gr. 4-6 |
| SSB1-90 | Seeds & Weeds Gr. 2-3 |
| SSY1-02 | Sentence Writing Gr. 1-3 |
| SST1-07A | September JK/SK |
| SST1-07B | September Gr. 1 |
| SST1-07C | September Gr. 2-3 |
| SSN1-30 | Serendipity Series Gr. 3-5 |
| SSC1-22 | Shamrocks on Parade Gr. 1 |
| SSC1-24 | Shamrocks, Harps & Shillelaghs 3-4 |
| SSR1-66 | Shakespeare Shorts-Perf Arts Gr. 1-4 |
| SSR1-67 | Shakespeare Shorts-Perf Arts Gr. 4-6 |
| SSR1-68 | Shakespeare Shorts-Lang Arts Gr. 2-4 |
| SSR1-69 | Shakespeare Shorts-Lang Arts Gr. 4-6 |
| SSB1-74 | Sharks Gr. 4-6 |
| SSN1-158 | Shiloh NS Gr. 4-6 |
| SSN1-84 | Sideways Stories Wayside NS 4-6 |
| SSN1-181 | Sight Words Activities Gr. 1 |
| SSB1-99 | Simple Machines Gr. 4-6 |
| SSN1-19 | Sixth Grade Secrets 4-6 |
| SSG1-04 | Skill Building with Slates Gr. K-8 |
| SSN1-118 | Skinny Bones NS Gr. 4-6 |
| SSB1-24 | Skunks Gr. 3-5 |
| SSN1-191 | Sky is Falling NS Gr. 4-6 |
| SSB1-83 | Slugs & Snails Gr. 1-3 |
| SSB1-55 | Snakes Gr. 4-6 |
| SST1-12A | Snow Gr. JK/SK |
| SST1-12B | Snow Gr. 1 |
| SST1-12C | Snow Gr. 2-3 |
| SSB1-76 | Solar System Gr. 4-6 |
| SSPC-44 | South America B/W Pictures |
| SSA1-11 | South America Gr. 4-6 |
| SSB1-05 | Space Gr. 2-3 |
| SSR1-34 | Spelling Blacklines Gr. 1 |
| SSR1-35 | Spelling Blacklines Gr. 2 |
| SSR1-14 | Spelling Gr. 1 |
| SSR1-15 | Spelling Gr. 2 |
| SSR1-16 | Spelling Gr. 3 |
| SSR1-17 | Spelling Gr. 4 |
| SSR1-18 | Spelling Gr. 5 |
| SSR1-19 | Spelling Gr. 6 |
| SSR1-27 | Spelling Worksavers #1 Gr. 3-5 |
| SSM1-02 | Spring Celebration Gr. 2-3 |
| SST1-01A | Spring Gr. JK/SK |
| SST1-01B | Spring Gr. 1 |
| SST1-01C | Spring Gr. 2-3 |
| SSM1-01 | Spring in the Garden Gr. 1-2 |
| SSB1-26 | Squirrels Gr. 3-5 |
| SSB1-112 | Stable Structures & Mechanisms 3 |
| SSG1-05 | Steps in the Research Process 5-8 |
| SSG1-02 | Stock Market Gr. 7-8 |
| SSN1-139 | Stone Fox NS Gr. 4-6 |
| SSN1-214 | Stone Orchard NS Gr. 7-8 |
| SSN1-01 | Story Book Land of Witches Gr. 2-3 |
| SSR1-64 | Story Starters Gr. 1-3 |
| SSR1-65 | Story Starters Gr. 4-6 |
| SSR1-73 | Story Starters Gr. 1-6 |
| SSY1-09 | Story Writing Gr. 1-3 |
| SSB1-111 | Structures, Mechanisms & Motion 2 |
| SSN1-211 | Stuart Little NS Gr. 4-6 |
| SSK1-29 | Subtraction Drills Gr. 1-3 |
| SSY1-05 | Subtraction Gr. 1-3 |
| SSY1-11 | Successful Language Pract. Gr. 1-3 |
| SSY1-12 | Successful Math Practice Gr. 1-3 |
| SSW1-09 | Summer Learning Gr. K-1 |
| SSW1-10 | Summer Learning Gr. 1-2 |
| SSW1-11 | Summer Learning Gr. 2-3 |
| SSW1-12 | Summer Learning Gr. 3-4 |
| SSW1-13 | Summer Learning Gr. 4-5 |
| SSW1-14 | Summer Learning Gr. 5-6 |
| SSN1-159 | Summer of the Swans NS Gr. 4-6 |
| SSZ1-02 | Summer Olympics Gr. 4-6 |
| SSM1-07 | Super Summer Gr. 1-2 |
| SSN1-18 | Superfudge NS Gr. 4-6 |
| SSA1-08 | Switzerland Gr. 4-6 |
| SSN1-20 | T.V. Kid NS. Gr. 4-6 |
| SSA1-15 | Take a Trip to Australia Gr. 2-3 |
| SSB1-102 | Taking Off With Flight Gr. 1-3 |
| SSN1-259 | Tale of Despereaux Gr. 4-6 |
| SSN1-55 | Tales of the Fourth Grade NS 4-6 |
| SSN1-188 | Taste of Blackberries NS Gr. 4-6 |
| SSK1-07 | Teaching Math Through Sports 6-9 |
| SST1-09A | Thanksgiving JK/SK |
| SST1-09C | Thanksgiving Gr. 2-3 |
| SSN1-77 | There's a Boy in the Girls... NS 4-6 |
| SSN1-143 | This Can't Be Happening NS 4-6 |
| SSN1-05 | Three Billy Goats Gruff NS Gr. 1-3 |
| SSN1-72 | Ticket to Curlew NS Gr. 4-6 |
| SSN1-82 | Timothy of the Cay NS Gr. 7-8 |
| SSF1-32 | Titanic Gr. 4-6 |
| SSN1-222 | To Kill a Mockingbird NS Gr. 7-8 |
| SSN1-195 | Toilet Paper Tigers NS Gr. 4-6 |
| SSJ1-35 | Toronto Gr. 4-8 |
| SSH1-02 | Toy Shelf Gr. P-K |
| SSPC-24 | Toys B/W Pictures |
| SSN1-163 | Traditional Poetry Gr. 7-10 |
| SSH1-13 | Transportation Gr. 4-6 |
| SSW1-01 | Transportation Snip Art |
| SSB1-03 | Trees Gr. 2-3 |
| SSA1-01 | Tropical Rainforest Gr. 4-6 |
| SSN1-56 | Trumpet of the Swan NS Gr. 4-6 |
| SSN1-81 | Tuck Everlasting NS Gr. 4-6 |
| SSN1-126 | Turtles in Literature Gr. 1-3 |
| SSN1-45 | Underground to Canada NS 4-6 |
| SSN1-27 | Unicorns in Literature Gr. 3-5 |
| SSJ1-44 | Upper & Lower Canada Gr. 7-8 |
| SSN1-192 | Using Novels Canadian North Gr. 7-8 |
| SSC1-14 | Valentines Day Gr. 5-8 |
| SSPC-45 | Vegetables B/W Pictures |
| SSY1-01 | Very Hungry Caterpillar NS 30/Pkg 1-3 |
| SSF1-13 | Victorian Era Gr. 7-8 |
| SSC1-35 | Victorian Christmas Gr. 5-8 |
| SSF1-17 | Viking Age Gr. 4-6 |
| SSN1-206 | War with Grandpa SN Gr. 4-6 |
| SSB1-91 | Water Gr. 2-4 |
| SSN1-166 | Watership Down NS Gr. 7-8 |
| SSH1-16 | Ways We Travel Gr. P-K |
| SSN1-101 | Wayside Sch. Little Stranger NS 4-6 |
| SSN1-76 | Wayside Sch. is Falling Down NS 4-6 |
| SSB1-60 | Weather Gr. 4-6 |
| SSN1-17 | Wee Folk in Literature Gr. 3-5 |
| SSPC-08 | Weeds B/W Pictures |
| SSQ1-04 | Welcome Back – Big Book Pkg 1-3 |
| SSB1-73 | Whale Preservation Gr. 5-8 |
| SSH1-08 | What is a Community? Gr. 2-4 |
| SSH1-01 | What is a Family? Gr. 2-3 |
| SSH1-09 | What is a School? Gr. 1-2 |
| SSJ1-32 | What is Canada? Gr. P-K |
| SSN1-79 | What is RAD? Read & Discover 2-4 |
| SSB1-62 | What is the Weather Today? Gr. 2-4 |
| SSN1-194 | What's a Daring Detective NS 4-6 |
| SSH1-10 | What's My Number Gr. P-K |
| SSR1-02 | What's the Scoop on Words Gr. 4-6 |
| SSN1-73 | Where the Red Fern Grows NS 7-8 |
| SSN1-87 | Where the Wild Things Are NS 1-3 |

# Publication Listing

| Code # | Title and Grade |
|--------|-----------------|
| SSN1-187 | Whipping Boy NS Gr. 4-6 |
| SSN1-226 | Who is Frances Rain? NS Gr. 4-6 |
| SSN1-74 | Who's Got Gertie & How...? NS 4-6 |
| SSN1-131 | Why did the Underwear ... NS 4-6 |
| SSC1-28 | Why Wear a Poppy? Gr. 2-3 |
| SSJ1-11 | Wild Animals of Canada Gr. 2-3 |
| SSPC-07 | Wild Flowers B/W Pictures |
| SSB1-18 | Winter Birds Gr. 2-3 |
| SSZ1-03 | Winter Olympics Gr. 4-6 |
| SSM1-04 | Winter Wonderland Gr. 1 |
| SSC1-01 | Witches Gr. 3-4 |
| SSN1-213 | Wolf Island NS Gr. 1-3 |
| SSE1-09 | Wolfgang Amadeus Mozart 6-9 |
| SSB1-23 | Wolves Gr. 3-5 |
| SSC1-20 | Wonders of Easter Gr. 2 |
| SSB1-35 | World of Horses Gr. 4-6 |
| SSB1-13 | World of Pets Gr. 2-3 |
| SSF1-26 | World War II Gr. 7-8 |
| SSN1-221 | Wrinkle in Time NS Gr. 7-8 |
| SSPC-02 | Zoo Animals B/W Pictures |
| SSB1-08 | Zoo Animals Gr. 1-2 |
| SSB1-09 | Zoo Celebration Gr. 3-4 |